Brothers and Sisters to Us

GW00992342

**U.S. Bishops'
Pastoral Letter on
Racism in Our Day**

November 14, 1979
United States Catholic Conference

U.S. BISHOPS' PASTORAL LETTER ON RACISM IN OUR DAY

November 14, 1979

Racism is an evil which endures in our society and in our Church. Despite apparent advances and even significant changes in the last two decades, the reality of racism remains. In large part it is only the external appearances which have changed.

In 1958 we spoke out against the blatant forms of racism that divided people through discriminatory laws and enforced segregation. We pointed out the moral evil that denied human persons their dignity as children of God and their God-given rights.[1] A decade later in a second pastoral letter we again underscored the continuing scandal of racism and called for decisive action to eradicate it from our society.[2]

We recognize and applaud the readiness of many Americans to make new strides forward in reducing and eliminating prejudice against minorities. We are convinced that the majority of Americans realize that racial discrimination is both unjust and unworthy of this nation.

We do not deny that changes have been made, that laws have been passed, that policies have been implemented. We do not deny that the ugly external features of racism which marred our society have in part been eliminated. But neither can it be denied that too often what has happened has been only a covering over, not a fundamental change. Today the sense of urgency has yielded to an apparent acceptance of the status quo. The climate of crisis engendered by demonstrations, protests, and confrontation has given way to a mood of indifference; and other issues occupy our attention.

In response to this mood, we wish to call attention to the persistent presence of racism and in particular to the relationship between racial and economic justice. Racism and economic oppression are distinct but interrelated forces which dehumanize our society. Movement toward authentic justice demands a simultaneous attack on both evils. Our economic structures are undergoing fundamental changes which threaten to intensify social inequalities in our nation. We are entering an era characterized by limited resources, restricted job markets and dwindling revenues.

---

[1]*Discrimination and Christian Conscience.* National Catholic Welfare Conference. 1958.

[2]*National Race Crisis.* National Conference of Catholic Bishops. 1968.

In this atmosphere, the poor and racial minorities are being asked to bear the heaviest burden of the new economic pressures.

This new economic crisis reveals an unresolved racism that permeates our society's structures and resides in the hearts of many among the majority. Because it is less blatant, this subtle form of racism is in some respects even more dangerous—harder to combat and easier to ignore. Major segments of the population are being pushed to the margins of society in our nation. As economic pressures tighten, those people who are often black, Hispanic, Native American and Asian—and always poor—slip further into the unending cycle of poverty, deprivation, ignorance, disease, and crime. Racial identity is for them an iron curtain barring the way to a decent life and livelihood. The economic pressures exacerbate racism, particularly where poor white people are competing with minorities for limited job opportunities. The Church must not be unmindful of these economic pressures. We must be sensitive to the unfortunate and unnecessary racial tension that results from this kind of economic need.

Mindful of its duty to be the advocate for those who hunger and thirst for justice's sake, the Church cannot remain silent about the racial injustices in society and in its own structures. Our concern over racism follows, as well, from our strong commitment to evangelization. Pope John Paul II has defined evangelization as bringing consciences, both individual and social, into conformity with the Gospel.[3] We would betray our commitment to evangelize ourselves and our society were we not to strongly voice our condemnation of attitudes and practices so contrary to the Gospel. Therefore, as the bishops of the United States, we once again address our pastoral reflections on racism to our brothers and sisters of all races.

We do this, conscious of the fact that racism is only one form of discrimination that infects our society. Such discrimination belies both our civil and religious traditions. The United States of America rests on a constitutional heritage that recognizes the equality, dignity, and inalienable rights of all its citizens. Further, we are heirs of a religious teaching which proclaims that all men and women, as children of God, are brothers and sisters. Every form of discrimination against individuals and groups—whether because of race, ethnicity, religion, gender, economic status, or national or cultural origin—is a serious injustice which has severely weakened our social fabric and deprived our country of the unique contributions of many of our citizens. While cognizant of these broader concerns, we wish to draw attention here to the particular form of discrimination that is based on race.

---

[3]Pope John Paul II Address at the Third General Assembly of The Latin American Bishops, Puebla, Mexico, January 28, 1979, p. 1.2.

THE SIN OF RACISM

Racism is a sin: a sin that divides the human family, blots out the image of God among specific members of that family, and violates the fundamental human dignity of those called to be children of the same Father. Racism is the sin that says some human beings are inherently superior and others essentially inferior because of race. It is the sin that makes racial characteristics the determining factor for the exercise of human rights. It mocks the words of Jesus: "Treat others the way you would have them treat you."[4] Indeed, racism is more than a disregard for the words of Jesus; it is a denial of the truth of the dignity of each human being revealed by the mystery of the Incarnation.

In order to find the strength to overcome the evil of racism, we must look to Christ. In Christ Jesus "there does not exist among you Jew or Greek, slave or freeman, male or female. All are one in Christ Jesus."[5] As Pope John Paul II has said so clearly, "Our spirit is set in one direction, the only direction for our intellect, will and heart is—toward Christ our Redeemer, toward Christ, the Redeemer of [humanity.]"[6] It is in Christ, then, that the Church finds the central cause for its commitment to justice, and to the struggle for the human rights and dignity of all persons.

When we give in to our fears of the other because he or she is of a race different from ourselves, when we prejudge the motives of others precisely because they are of a different color, when we stereotype or ridicule the other because of racial characteristics and heritage, we fail to heed the command of the Prophet Amos: "Seek good and not evil, that you may live; then truly will the Lord . . . be with you as you claim! . . . Then let justice surge like water, and goodness like an unfailing stream."[7]

Today in our country men, women, and children are being denied opportunities for full participation and advancement in our society because of their race. The educational, legal, and financial systems, along with other structures and sectors of our society, impede people's progress and narrow their access because they are black, Hispanic, Native American or Asian.

The structures of our society are subtly racist, for these structures reflect the values which society upholds. They are geared to the success of the majority and the failure of the minority. Members of both groups give unwitting approval by accepting things as they are. Perhaps no single individual is to blame. The sinfulness is often anonymous but nonetheless real. The sin is social in nature

---

[4]Matthew, 7:12.

[5]Galatians, 3:28.

[6]Redemptor Hominis, 7. Pope John Paul II. 1979.

[7]Amos, 5:14, 24.

in that each of us, in varying degrees, is responsible. All of us in some measure are accomplices. As our recent pastoral letter on moral values states: "The absence of personal fault for an evil does not absolve one of all responsibility. We must seek to resist and undo injustices we have not caused, lest we become bystanders who tacitly endorse evil and so share in guilt for it."[8]

RACISM IS A FACT

Because the Courts have eliminated statutory racial discrimination and Congress has enacted civil rights legislation, and because some minority people have achieved some measure of success, many people believe that racism is no longer a problem in American life. The continuing existence of racism becomes apparent, however, when we look beneath the surface of our national life: as, for example, in the case of unemployment figures. In the second quarter of 1979, 4.9% of white Americans were unemployed; but for blacks the figure was 11.6%; for Hispanics, 8.3%; and for Native Americans on reservations, as high as 40%. The situation is even more disturbing when one realizes that 35% of black youth, 19.1% of Hispanic youth, and an estimated 60% of Native American youth are unemployed.[9] Quite simply, this means that an alarming proportion of tomorrow's adults are cut off from gainful employment—an essential prerequisite of responsible adulthood. These same youths presently suffer the crippling effects of a segregated educational system which in many cases fails to enlighten the mind and free the spirit, which too often inculcates a conviction of inferiority and which frequently graduates persons who are ill-prepared and inadequately trained. In addition, racism raises its ugly head in the violence that frequently surrounds attempts to achieve racial balance in education and housing.

With respect to family life, we recognize that decades of denied access to opportunities have been for minority families a crushing burden. Racial discrimination has only exacerbated the harmful relationship between poverty and family instability.

Racism is only too apparent in housing patterns in our major cities and suburbs. Witness the deterioration of inner cities and the segregation of many suburban areas by means of unjust practices of social steering and blockbusting. Witness also the high proportion of Hispanics, blacks, and Indians on welfare and the fact that the median income of nonwhite families is only 63% of the

---

[8]*To Live in Christ Jesus,* p. 25. National Conference of Catholic Bishops. 1976.

[9]*Employment and Earnings,* Vol. 26, No. 10, Dept. of Labor, Bureau of Labor Statistics, October, 1979. Precise data on youth unemployment among Native Americans are not available. The 60% unemployment figure is an estimate by the U.S. Dept. of Labor.

average white family income. Moreover, the gap between the rich and the poor is widening, not decreasing.[10]

Racism is apparent when we note that the population in our prisons consists disproportionately of minorities; that violent crime is the daily companion of a life of poverty and deprivation; and that the victims of such crimes are also disproportionately nonwhite and poor. Racism is also apparent in the attitudes and behavior of some law enforcement officials and in the unequal availability of legal assistance.

Finally, racism is sometimes apparent in the growing sentiment that too much is being given to racial minorities by way of affirmative action programs or allocations to redress long-standing imbalances in minority representation and government-funded programs for the disadvantaged. At times, protestations claiming that all persons should be treated equally reflect the desire to maintain a *status quo* that favors one race and social group at the expense of the poor and the nonwhite.

Racism obscures the evils of the past and denies the burdens that history has placed upon the shoulders of our black, Hispanic, Native American, and Asian brothers and sisters. An honest look at the past makes plain the need for restitution wherever possible—makes evident the justice of restoration and redistribution.

A LOOK AT THE PAST

Racism has been part of the social fabric of America since its European colonization. Whether it be the tragic past of the Native Americans, the Mexicans, the Puerto Ricans, or the blacks, the story is one of slavery, peonage, economic exploitation, brutal repression, and cultural neglect. All have suffered indignity; most have been uprooted, defrauded or dispossessed of their lands; and none have escaped one or another form of collective degradation by a powerful majority. Our history is littered with the debris of broken promises and treaties, as well as lynchings and massacres that almost destroyed the Indians, humiliated the Hispanics, and crushed the blacks.

But despite this tragic history, the racial minorities of our country have survived and increased. Each racial group has sunk its roots deep in the soil of our culture, thus helping to give to the United States its unique character and its diverse coloration. The contribution of each racial minority is distinctive and rich; each is a source of internal strength for our nation. The history of all gives a witness to a truth absorbed by now into the collective conscious-

---

[10] *Widening Economic Gap,* National Urban League, Research Dept., 1979. See also "Consumer Income," Current Population Report, Series P60 #118, 1979.

ness of Americans: their struggle has been a pledge of liberty and a challenge to future greatness.

RACISM TODAY

Crude and blatant expressions of racist sentiment, though they occasionally exist, are today considered bad form. Yet racism itself persists in covert ways. Under the guise of other motives, it is manifest in the tendency to stereotype and marginalize whole segments of the population whose presence is perceived as a threat. It is manifest also in the indifference that replaces open hatred. The minority poor are seen as the dross of a post-industrial society—without skills, without motivation, without incentive. They are expendable. Many times the new face of racism is the computer print-out, the graph of profits and losses, the pink slip, the nameless statistic. Today's racism flourishes in the triumph of private concern over public responsibility, individual success over social commitment, and personal fulfillment over authentic compassion. Then too, we recognize that racism also exists in the attitudes and behavior of some who are themselves members of minority groups. Christian ideals of justice must be brought to bear in both the private and the public sector in order that covert racism be eliminated wherever it exists.

The new forms of racism must be brought face-to-face with the figure of Christ. It is Christ's word that is the judgment on this world; it is Christ's cross that is the measure of our response; and it is Christ's face that is the composite of all persons but in a most significant way of today's poor, today's marginal people, today's minorities.

GOD'S JUDGMENT AND PROMISE

THE VOICE OF SCRIPTURE

The Christian response to the challenges of our times is to be found in the Good News of Jesus. The words that signaled the start of His public ministry must be the watchword for every Christian response to injustice, "He unrolled the scroll and found the passage where it was written: The spirit of the Lord is upon me; therefore, he has anointed me. He has sent me to bring glad tidings to the poor, to proclaim liberty to captives, recovery of sight to the blind and release to prisoners, to announce a year of favor from the Lord. Rolling up the scroll he gave it back . . . and sat down. . . . 'Today this Scripture passage is fulfilled in your hearing'."[11]

God's word proclaims the oneness of the human family—from the first words of Genesis, to the "Come, Lord Jesus" of the Book

---

[11]Luke, 4:17-21.

6

of Revelation. God's word in Genesis announces that all men and women are created in God's image; not just *some* races and racial types, but *all* bear the imprint of the Creator and are enlivened by the breath of His one Spirit.

In proclaiming the liberation of Israel, God's word proclaims the liberation of all people from slavery. God's word further proclaims that all people are accountable to and for each other. This is the message of that great parable of the Final Judgment: "When the Son of Man comes in his glory, escorted by all the angels of heaven . . . all the nations will be assembled before him. Then he will separate them into two groups. . . . The king will say to those on his right: 'Come. You have my Father's blessing! . . . For I was hungry and you gave me food, I was thirsty and you gave me drink. I was a stranger and you welcomed me. . . . I assure you, as often as you did it for one of my least brothers, you did it for me.' "[12]

God's word proclaims that the person "who listens to God's word but does not put it into practice is like a man who looks into a mirror at the face he was born with . . . then goes off and promptly forgets what he looked like."[13] We have forgotten that we "are strangers and aliens no longer. . . . [We] are fellow citizens of the saints and members of the household of God. [We] form a building which rises on the foundation of the apostles and prophets, with Christ Jesus himself as the capstone."[14]

THE VOICE OF THE CHURCH

This is the mystery of our Church, that all men and women are brothers and sisters, all one in Christ, all bear the image of the Eternal God. The Church is truly universal, embracing all races, for it is "the visible sacrament of this saving unity.[15] The Church, moreover, follows the example of its founder and, "through its children, is one with [people] of every condition, but especially with the poor and the afflicted."[16]

This Church has a duty to proclaim the truth about the human being as disclosed in the truth about Jesus Christ. As our Holy Father Pope John Paul II has written: "On account of the mystery of the Redemption [every human being] is entrusted to the solicitude of the Church." The human being is "the primary and fundamental way for the Church."[17]

---

[12]Matthew, 25:31-40.

[13]James, 1:23-24.

[14]Ephesians, 2:19-20.

[15]*Dogmatic Constittuion on the Church*, 9.

[16]*Decree on the Church's Missionary Activity*, 12.

[17]*Redemptor Hominis*, 13, 14.

It is important to realize in the case of racism that we are dealing with a distortion at the very heart of human nature. The ultimate remedy against evils such as this will not come solely from human effort. What is needed is the recreation of the human being according to the image revealed in Jesus Christ. For He reveals in himself what each human being can and must become.

How great, therefore, is that sin of racism which weakens the Church's witness as the universal sign of unity among all peoples! How great the scandal given by racist Catholics who would make the Body of Christ, the Church, a sign of racial oppression! Yet all too often the Church in our country has been for many a "white Church," a racist institution.

Each of us as Catholics must acknowledge a share in the mistakes and sins of the past. Many of us have been prisoners of fear and prejudice. We have preached the Gospel while closing our eyes to the racism it condemns. We have allowed conformity to social pressures to replace compliance with social justice.

But past mistakes must not hinder the Church's response to the challenges of the present. Worldwide, the Church today is not just European and American; it is also African, Asian, Indian, and Oceanic. It is western, eastern, northern and southern, black and also brown, white and also red and yellow. In our own country, one quarter of the Catholics are Spanish-speaking. A million black Catholics make Catholicism one of the largest denominations among black Americans today. Among our nation's original inhabitants, the Native Americans, the Church's presence is increasingly becoming developed and expressed within the cultures of the various Native American tribes.

It is a fact that Catholic dioceses and religious communities across the country for years have committed selected personnel and substantial funds to relieve oppression and to correct injustices and have striven to bring the Gospel to the diverse racial groups in our land. The Church has sought to aid the poor and downtrodden, who for the most part are also the victims of racial oppression. But this relationship has been and remains two-sided and reciprocal; for the initiative of racial minorities, clinging to their Catholic faith, has helped the Church to grow, adapt, and become truly Catholic and remarkably diverse. Today in our own land the face of Catholicism is the face of all humanity—a face of many colors, a countenance of many cultural forms.

Yet more is needed. The prophetic voice of the Church, which is to be heard in every generation and even to the ends of the earth, must not be muted—especially not by the counter witness of some of its own people. Let the Church speak out, not only in the assemblies of the bishops, but in every diocese and parish in the land, in every chapel and religious house, in every school, in every social service agency, and in every institution that bears the name Catholic. As Pope John Paul II has proclaimed, the Church must be aware of the threats to humanity and of all that opposes the endeavor to make life itself more human. The Church must strive to make every element of human life correspond to the true dignity of the human person.[18] And during his recent visit to this country, Pope John Paul II discussed the direct implications of this for the Church in the United States:

"It will always remain one of the glorious achievements of this nation that, when people looked toward America, they received together with freedom also a chance for their own advancement. This tradition must be honored also today. The freedom that was gained must be ratified each day by the firm rejection of whatever wounds, weakens or dishonors human life. And so I appeal to all who love freedom and justice to give a chance to all in need, to the poor and the powerless. Break open the hopeless cycles of poverty and ignorance that are still the lot of too many of our brothers and sisters; the hopeless cycles of prejudices that linger on despite enormous progress toward effective equality in education and employment; the cycles of despair in which are imprisoned all those that lack decent food, shelter or employment. . . ."[19]

Therefore, let the Church proclaim to all that the sin of racism defiles the image of God and degrades the sacred dignity of humankind which has been revealed by the mystery of the Incarnation. Let all know that it is a terrible sin that mocks the cross of Christ and ridicules the Incarnation. For the brother and sister of our Brother Jesus Christ are brother and sister to us.

THE VOICE OF THE WORLD

We find God's will for us not only in the word of Scripture and in the teaching of his Church but also in the issues and events of secular society. "The Church . . . recognizes that worthy elements are found in today's social movements, especially an evolution toward unity, a process of wholesome socialization and of association in civic and economic realms."[20] Thus spoke the Church in the Second Vatican Council. That same Council urged the Church, especially the laity, to work in the temporal sphere on behalf of justice and the unity of humankind.[21]

---

[18] *Redemptor Hominis,* 14.

[19] Homily at Battery Park, New York. Pope John Paul II. October, 1979.

[20] *Pastoral Constitution on the Church in the Modern World,* 42.

[21] *Pastoral Constitution on the Church in the Modern World,* 43.

With this in mind, we pay special tribute to those who have struggled and struggle today for civil rights and economic justice in our own country. Nor do we overlook the United Nations' Universal Declaration of Human Rights which still speaks to the conscience of the entire world and the several international covenants which demand the elimination of discrimination based on race. None of these, unfortunately, have been ratified by our country, whereas we in America should have been the first to do so. All have a duty to heed the voice of God speaking in these documents.

OUR RESPONSE

Racism is not merely one sin among many; it is a radical evil that divides the human family and denies the new creation of a redeemed world. To struggle against it demands an equally radical transformation, in our own minds and hearts as well as in the structure of our society.

Conversion is the ever present task of each Christian. In offering certain guidelines for this change of heart as it pertains to racism, we note that these are only first steps in what ought to be a continuing dialogue throughout the Catholic community and the nation at large. In this context we would urge that existing programs and plans, such as those dealing with family ministry, parish renewal, and evangelization, be used as vehicles for implementing the measures addressed here.

OUR PERSONAL LIVES

To the extent that racial bias affects our personal attitudes and judgments, to the extent that we allow another's race to influence our relationship and limit our openness, to the extent that we see yet close our hearts to our brothers and sisters in need,[22]—to that extent we are called to conversion and renewal in love and justice.

As individuals we should try to influence the attitudes of others by expressly rejecting racial stereotypes, racial slurs and racial jokes. We should influence the members of our families, especially our children, to be sensitive to the authentic human values and cultural contributions of each racial grouping in our country.

We should become more sensitive ourselves and thereby sensitize our acquaintances by learning more about how social structures inhibit the economic, educational, and social advancement of the poor. We should make a personal commitment to join with others in political efforts to bring about justice for the victims of such deprivation.

---

[22]I John, 3:17.

OUR CHURCH COMMUNITY

The Church must be constantly attentive to the Lord's voice as He calls on His people daily not to harden their hearts.[23] We urge that on all levels the Catholic Church in the United States examine its conscience regarding attitudes and behavior toward blacks, Hispanics, Native Americans, and Asians. We urge consideration of the evil of racism as it exists in the local Church and reflection upon the means of combatting it. We urge scrupulous attention at every level to insure that minority representation goes beyond mere tokenism and involves authentic sharing in responsibility and decision making.

We encourage Catholics to join hands with members of other religious groups in the spirit of ecumenism to achieve the common objectives of justice and peace. During the struggle for legal recognition of racial justice, an important chapter in American history was written as religious groups, Jewish, Protestant, and Catholic, joined in support of a civil rights movement which found much of its initiative and inspiration within the black Protestant Churches. This cooperation should continue to serve as a model for our times.

All too often in the very places where blacks, Hispanics, Native Americans, and Asians are numerous, the Church's officials and representatives, both clerical and lay, are predominantly white. Efforts to achieve racial balance in government, the media, the armed services, and other crucial areas of secular life should not only be supported but surpassed in the institutions and programs of the Catholic Church.

Particular care should be taken to foster vocations among minority groups.[24] Training for the priesthood, the permanent diaconate, and religious life should not entail an abandonment of culture and traditions or a loss of racial identity but should seek ways in which such culture and traditions might contribute to that training. Special attention is required whenever it is necessary to correct racist attitudes or behavior among seminary staff and seminarians. Seminary education ought to include an awareness of the history and the contributions of minorities as well as an appreciation of the enrichment of the liturgical expression, especially at the local parish level, which can be found in their respective cultures.

We affirm the teaching of Vatican II on the liturgy by noting that "the liturgy is the summit toward which the activity of the

---

[23] Psalms, 94:8.

[24] Concern for vocations from minority groups and the preparation of priests to serve in a multi-cultural and multi-racial society has been previously expressed in *The Program for Priestly Formation,* which was developed and approved by the National Conference of Catholic Bishops, 1976.

Church is directed."[25] The Church must "respect and foster the spiritual . . . gifts of the various races and peoples"[26] and encourage the incorporation of these gifts into the liturgy.

We see the value of fostering greater diversity of racial and minority group representation in the hierarchy. Furthermore, we call for the adoption of an effective affirmative action program in every diocese and religious institution.

We strongly urge that special attention be directed to the plight of undocumented workers and that every effort be made to remove the fear and prejudice of which they are victims.

We ask in particular that Catholic institutions such as schools, universities, social service agencies, and hospitals, where members of racial minorities are often employed in large numbers, review their policies to see that they faithfully conform to the Church's teaching on justice for workers and respect for their rights. We recommend that investment portfolios be examined in order to determine whether racist institutions and policies are inadvertently being supported; and that, wherever possible, the capital of religious groups be made available for new forms of alternative investment, such as cooperatives, land trusts, and housing for the poor. We further recommend that Catholic institutions avoid the services of agencies and industries which refuse to take affirmative action to achieve equal opportunity and that the Church itself always be a model as an equal opportunity employer.

We recommend that leadership training programs be established on the local level in order to encourage effective leadership among racial minorities on all levels of the Church, local as well as national.

In particular, we recommend the active spiritual and financial support of associations and institutions organized by Catholic blacks, Hispanics, Native Americans, and Asians within the Church for the promotion of ministry to and by their respective communities. There is also need for more attention to finding ways in which minorities can work together across racial and cultural lines to avoid duplication and competition among themselves. There is also a need for cooperative efforts between racial minorities and other social action groups, such as labor and the women's movement.

Finally, we urgently recommend the continuation and expansion of Catholic schools in the inner cities and other disadvantaged areas. No other form of Christian ministry has been more widely acclaimed or desperately sought by leaders of various racial com-

---

[25]*Constitution on the Sacred Liturgy*, 10.

[26]*Constitution on the Sacred Liturgy*, 37.

munities. For a century and a half the Church in the United States has been distinguished by its efforts to educate the poor and disadvantaged, many of whom are not of the Catholic faith. That tradition continues today in—among other places—Catholic schools, where so many blacks, Hispanics, Native Americans, and Asians receive a form of education and formation which constitutes a key to greater freedom and dignity. It would be tragic if today, in the face of acute need and even near despair, the Church, for centuries the teacher and the guardian of civilization, should withdraw from this work in our own society. No sacrifice can be so great, no price can be so high, no short-range goals can be so important as to warrant the lessening of our commitment to Catholic education in minority neighborhoods. More affluent parishes should be made aware of this need and of their opportunity to share resources with the poor and needy in a way that recognizes the dignity of both giver and receiver.

SOCIETY AT LARGE

Individuals move on many levels in our complex society: each of us is called to speak and act in many different settings. In each case may we speak and act according to our competence and as the Gospel bids us. With this as our prayer, we refrain from giving detailed answers to complex questions on which we ourselves have no special competence. Instead, we propose several guidelines of a general nature.

The difficulties of these new times demand a new vision and a renewed courage to transform our society and achieve justice for all. We must fight for the dual goals of racial and economic justice with determination and creativity. Domestically, justice demands that we strive for authentic full employment, recognizing the special need for employment of those who, whether men or women, carry the principal responsibility for support of a family. Justice also demands that we strive for decent working conditions, adequate income, housing, education, and health care for all. Government at the national and local levels must be held accountable by all citizens for the essential services which all are entitled to receive. The private sector should work with various racial communities to insure that they receive a just share of the profits they have helped to create.

Globally, we live in an interdependent community of nations, some rich, some poor. Some are high consumers of the world's resources; some eke out an existence on a near starvation level. As it happens, most of the rich, consuming nations are white and Christian; most of the world's poor are of other races and religions.

Concerning our relationship to other nations, our Christian faith suggests several principles. First, racial difference should not interfere with our dealing justly and peacefully with all other nations. Secondly, those nations which possess more of the world's riches must, in justice, share with those who are in serious need. Finally, the private sector should be aware of its responsibility to promote racial justice, not subordination or exploitation, to promote genuine development in poor societies, not mere consumerism and materialism.

CONCLUSION

Our words here are an initial response to one of the major concerns which emerged during the consultation on social justice entitled "a Call to Action," which was part of the U.S. Catholic participation in the national bicentennial. The dialogue must continue among the Catholics of our country. We have proposed guidelines and principles and as the bishops of the Catholic Conference in the United States, we must give the leadership to this effort by a commitment of our time, of personnel and of significant financial resources. Others must develop the programs and plan operations. There must be no turning back along the road of justice, no sighing for bygone times of privilege, no nostalgia for simple solutions from another age. For we are children of the age to come, when the first shall be last and the last first, when blessed are they who serve Christ the Lord in all His brothers and sisters, especially those who are poor and suffer injustice.